THE
BLUFFER'S
THE ROCK BUSINESS

DAVID KNOPFLER

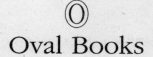

Oval Books

Published by Oval Books
335 Kennington Road
London SE11 4QE

Telephone (0) 20 7582 7123
Fax: (0) 20 7582 1022
E-mail: info@ovalbooks.com

First published by Ravette Publishing, 1996
First published by Oval Books, 2000

Series Editor – Anne Tauté

Cover designer – Jim Wire, Quantum
Printer – Cox & Wyman Ltd
Producer – Oval Projects Ltd

The Bluffer's Guides® series is based
on an original idea by Peter Wolfe.

The Bluffer's Guide®, The Bluffer's
Guides®, Bluffer's®, and Bluff Your
Way® are Registered Trademarks.

Dedicated to Anna

With acknowledgement to Bill Flanagan,
and thanks to Harry Bogdanovs for his
unique insight into Juke Box icongraphy.

ISBN: 1-903096-17-0

CONTENTS

GETTING STARTED, GETTING IN

The first decision a budding bluffer seeking a career in the music business will need to make is whether to:

a) become a recording artist, or
b) forge a career in one of the many other areas of the music business – session musician, management, record production, marketing, advertising, broadcasting, music publishing and so forth.

It's a mysterious fact to the outside observer that those with a real talent for making music rarely wind up as recording artists, whereas those with no apparent talent for it can frequently be found at the top of the charts.

The Recording Artist

You do not need special talent to become a recording artist. You only need one thing, and that is a recording contract. Unfortunately a real recording contract (one that genuinely means you'll get to make records that will be commercially released worldwide) are very hard to come by. Once however you have done the **Deal** (see The Deal and How to Survive It) you will be over the first major hurdle and well on your way to becoming completely disillusioned with the one thing that probably brought you into this industry – the one thing that nobody really knows too much about – music.

Like Alice in Wonderland, nothing in the rock music business is what it seems. Record companies vary from one solitary bass player in the suburbs who sells his guitar to buy a limited trading company and fancies himself as a record mogul, to the global giants like Time Warner, who are able to confidently command debt burdens greater than most Western nations, and which some might argue make the US government appear to be the soul of probity.

Assuming that you are not intimately connected to the president of a real record label (i.e. one with more than two personnel and large sums of money to spend) and cannot buy him lunch or lose at golf to him, your next best approach is, unfortunately, through **A&R**.

The kind of music you propose to make is not really too much of a consideration; providing you understand the traditional method of obtaining a record deal – that you are able to bluff and that your demo does not sound anything like music (as it is usually understood) – you are already well on your way to finding yourself being played with positive enthusiasm in the hallowed portals of the A&R man. A&R personnel are usually, but not always, men, and rock 'n roll being the last sanctioned bastion of sexism means they almost always have young female secretaries. Once such a secretary pins up the photograph of a burgeoning rock-god on her wall, you can confidently start announcing that a deal is imminent.

Remember that PROFILE is always more important than music. If you currently enjoy a successful career as a soap star, or have a role in a TV drama series, your chances of getting a deal rise considerably. Alternatively, try finding a way to be at the centre of a controversy likely to be covered by the tabloid press, provided the consequence is not likely to involve long periods in jail or threaten green card status further down the road. Try, if at all possible, to

6

be under twenty years of age. Photogenic qualities are certainly an advantage, but stylistically should not, at this stage, be too evident. That your looks will lend themselves to extensive professional remoulding is enough.

The aspiring rock star should either go with the flow or run against it, but never try to do both. If you start out on the rock circuit with a bad attitude, then comprehensively cultivate it. Keith Richards has always, for example, been a role model for NME (Enemy) readers, whereas Cliff Richard...

When record company executives at the hotel bar confide the sordid, intimate secrets about their artists, or indeed a rival label's artist, as sooner or later they will if you spend any time in such places, these invariably fall into one of three categories:

1. Great guys.
2. Degenerates, junkies, killers, perverts, and pædophiles.
3. Difficult artists.

If, as a recording artist, you have sunk all the way down to category three, you are in big trouble. If you started your career there that's a tougher break: a career in politics or social work would be a step up. It should not be an objective, but it may be of some consolation to know that many songwriters of respectable pedigree before you have resided either there or in therapy, usually both.

Great guys don't move around one leg in front of the other like normal folk, they breeze everywhere, making witty and positive remarks to everyone. It's always a party around a great guy, which is why they have to sod off to recover as fast as their elevator shoes allow, the minute their minders can find them a diplomatic exit. Autographs for them are an opportunity to 'meet their fans', and this could include heads of corporations, radio bosses, TV producers, as well as the usual sprinkling of fame spotters generally found outside most TV studios – particularly prevalent in Germany. When the Germans say "You will sign my cards" they are actually saying "You will sign my cards?". Unfortunately the question mark often gets lost in the translation and degenerates are quite likely to say, in riposte, "Are you related to Mark Chapman? Piss off, you sad creep", especially if it's patently obvious that incipient 'stalkers' have no idea who the artist is, and only want the autographs to flog to their lonely friends.

Nevertheless, the rising rock star should sign anything, anywhere, anytime, including body parts. Get that profile moving. Soon you will have progressed to carrying autographed photographs for just such occasions. By the time you are successful enough to be mobbed, there will be a fleet of people whose job it is to ensure that you are mobbed, and a second fleet of people employed to protect you if you are. Enjoy it for the three months it lasts.

Veteran bluffers are difficult but great guys who have overcome a major hurdle like a death, cancer, drug dependency, and so on. They will inspire pity and admiration in equal measure and have learned to live easily in all three categories simultaneously.

Etiquette

There are those who subscribe to the theory that since much of rock 'n roll's business methods originated with the New York hit men, contemporary manners can

8

therefore correspond to those of contemporary New Yorkers on a hot day. When someone doesn't return your calls, or your faxes, which, for most rock business people is the daily norm, it means exactly what it feels like. It means "Go away, you dull little @£$%^*". It means "We don't give a tuppenny %^&* about you, or the product you have to offer – at least not this month". This is depressing, if you let it be. However, there are consolations. The offending parties will, of course, ask solicitously about your welfare if obliged to interact with you in the future, but within six months they will probably have moved jobs, somewhere well below the rung of the ladder you are presently clinging to, like one who is about to be shipwrecked. Six more months and they might be out of the business altogether and taking their first stab at being a proper grown up.

The Manager

In order to communicate your street cred desires to the record company, you will need to share a percentage (normally around 15 to 20%) of all monies you can make with a shadowy figure known as the manager.

This is the person with whom the successful rock star will spend more time than the person they eventually marry and expensively divorce. Managers will know all the intimate secrets of how to be a complete bastard and everyone's friend at the same time. Governments may fall, countries may starve, but their act will get top billing.

Fear them or loathe them, the record company will need to deal with them. Certain managers may reach an almost legendary status, where they can appear to some to do no wrong. Normally loath to praise their peers, most rock managers would reluctantly concur that Steve O'Rourke's supervision of Pink Floyd's mega successful revival (despite their main composer and singer leaving) falls into this category. O'Rourke, undeterred by Roger Water's departure, secured the legal right for the remaining musicians to trade as Pink Floyd and steered a well-worn formula back to stadium touring with commensurate platinum sales and satellite global broadcasts.

Roger Davis's ability to revive Tina Turner's fortunes after a long spell in relative obscurity is another example. If one characteristic typifies what establishes quality rock management, it is the same quality which surrounds their artists – longevity, combined with platinum status record sales. This exclusive club of millionaires all have one thing in common: reasonably talented recording artists, luck, intelligence and a solid grasp of how to bluff your way in the music business.

A good rock manager is almost always a respected rock manager. A respected rock manager is almost always a rich and successful, fêted and hated, rock manager. A rich and successful rock manager has rich and successful artists. From the outside it appears seamless, as much of a conjuring trick as where they have stashed their undeclared earnings. Only one fact can be counted on. Enterprising rock managers will know with time-honoured bluffing skills that they must make their own achievements appear to be the solid accomplishments of their artists.

They will always know how to both stroke and kick the label, and even their artists, to get the effect they want from them. One noted manager memorised a floor plan (including names and desks) of the New York record company office so that when he visited he would know the first names of everyone there and announce them as he walked through. "Hi, Shelly. Good t' see ya again, Frank." The principle of being nice to the person who carries your bag is well understood in this business: next year he might turn up as the company's new head of promotions.

Memo to: The Ambitious Manager

Never expect your artists to appreciate what is being done for them. When they don't, remember that this is testament to your ability to convince them that their success is merely an act of divine judgement. Your bluff that your artists are 'simply the best' must convince not only the record label and all its personnel, but also the artists themselves.

The endless rota – of lunches, dinners, phone calls, schmoozing – is simply invisible to the young rock-god singer-songwriter struggling over his rhyming of 'rain' with 'pain'. If you've done your job properly, your artists will casually presume that you are simply a one-dimensional person with an irrational obsession for making them globally successful whilst remaining entirely honest, trustworthy and, above all, entertaining company. Don't disillusion them.

Avoiding the Usual Lies and Traps

You can't, so forget it.

THE RECORD COMPANY

Record companies divide into two camps – the **Majors** and the **Indies** (or Independent labels).

The Majors

Majors are record labels owned by multinational conglomerates, able to command apparently infinite resources endlessly financed by the world's stock markets.

To become a player in one of these companies does not require any ability whatsoever; however, to be a player of a musical instrument in one of these companies, or more precisely a failed musician, can prove more useful than a third class honours degree in law or accountancy. Every major has an in-house collective of hobbyist 'musicians' ready to rise to the challenge of meeting famous tennis players and novelists to ruin an otherwise perfectly decent social event – racing drivers being the latest in the scramble to get in on this fashion for professionals going amateur.

From the record company's standpoint, there are several varieties of real recording artists.

1. Those who make good records that make big money (extremely rare)
2. Those who make bad records that make good money (less rare)
3. Those who make bad records that lose lots of money (numerous)
4. Those who make good records that make no money (even more numerous).

Any self-respecting record company will endeavour, without much success, to sign only those artists that fit the first, or failing that, the second category, although failing to do so will not necessarily work against you provided you know a few simple stratagems which prevent failure sticking to you. Since this business is unique in that over 95% of its product fails to chart, and that most of its product doesn't make money, the lessons need to be rapidly learnt if one is to survive for long.

Remember, quality is always considered problematic: Arthouse – Intelligent – Minority – Cult – are all words that send most executives scuttling back behind closed doors for a quick burst of Meatloaf or Cher on their enormous out-of-phase speakers.

The size and type of a record company executive's hi-fi speaker is a subterfuge all of its own. The rule is either have the best speakers money can buy (even if not actually connected) or some banged-up ancient valve amp with the speakers at different heights and inappropriate positions in the room. This battered variety of hi-fi is usually to be found in the A&R rooms. The talent scout's preference for garage music that doesn't resemble anything the rest of us could begin to conceive of as a record is always a sure sign of an effective bluffer at work.

Never, unless you are the President, make the mistake of leaving the cloth fronts on your speakers. Having normal speakers could reveal that you don't frequent recording studios. Recording studios also practise 'naked' speakers as a ritual. That this practice evolved in the sixties to humour increasingly deaf electric guitarists who needed every ounce of clarity (and more particularly treble) going, just to hear anything at all, is not a witticism to repeat.

A record executive with legal training will always require bigger speakers than executives who were formerly musicians – that way everyone can see that they actually listen to music. In fact, executives never listen to music because they are always too busy on the phone spending their way out of trouble. Spending is the only sure-fire method that guarantees either a profit or a promotion to a rival company. Or, if they are really cunning, both.

The one who can give the impression of having a budget that is completely out of control whilst in reality being reasonably prudent is probably by now a master bluffer, and president of one of the tiny handful of majors.

The Indies

Indies used to be tiny record labels (sometimes no more than a vehicle for a self-financing band) which regularly went into liquidation faster than Michael Schumacher completing a lap on the Grand Prix circuit. These days, however, the picture is changing, because a number of indies have found ways of obtaining funds in some form or other from their bigger cousins, the majors, while still retaining some independence of operation. Now, when they go broke, they can sometimes jubilantly announce that they have been 'bought out' by a major. In reality the only way that their distributor, usually a major, can recoup their investment is by taking over the label into which they have been haemorrhaging money (through pressing plant bills, promo costs, unpaid distribution, design, video costs, etc.).

The main reasons that such a large number of tinier indies go spectacularly (or quietly) broke are that:

a) they can't re-finance with billions from the stock market like majors

b) not infrequently, they are owned by individuals who couldn't spread a sandwich unaided, let alone master a spread sheet, and who in all probability cannot afford to MOT their cars. These are people who think that overheads can be found above railway lines. One former record company, owned by a builder called Fred, who fancied owning a recording studio and meeting the stars, went broke because they forgot in their costing that on every record they sold they would need to pay between 6½-8% of the cake to the copyright collection agency who collect royalties for the song-writer. These royalties, known as 'mechanicals', are payable in some countries not just on every record sold but on every record pressed – which, when you find most of your stock being returned to your warehouse (or bedroom) from the record stores, unsold, will generally wipe you out pretty effortlessly.

c) the company has (or had) pots of money, but were not used to the shenanigans of the music biz, so were milked blind by all the indie sharks who operate little indie promo companies, and their ilk, which promise (but rarely deliver) hits in return for non-bouncing cash. So they wind up paying large advances for records which they then find they cannot afford to press. Generally, the lower the hit profile of a company, the more they will have to pay out to obtain artists of any status. Promise of personal attention is the usual bluff offered as an inducement to the disillusioned former star who has just suffered what he or she regards as severe indifference at the hands of a major which released the record, but forgot, or was unwilling, or unable, to promote and distribute it. The experience of having twenty plays a week on the highest rated national radio station, but all the stock locked up in a factory waiting for its bills to be paid, is not the scenario most indies plan for, but it happens.

There is a fail-safe method of judging the status of the record company you are interested in signing to – the Juke Box. This is a sacred icon of the hit man. You are unlikely to frequent music biz offices for long before encountering one of these dinosaurs. The quality of the juke box can speak volumes so you only need to know how to read the obvious signs these artifacts represent:

a) **Small replica Juke Boxes**. Companies with a small replica juke box may only be offering the opportunity of small replica careers.

b) **A Genuine Wurlitzer**. If it isn't in working condition, maybe it stopped because a recent metal signing celebration party led to the drummer pouring a bottle of Southern Comfort into the works to 'smooth things out'. Or maybe it hasn't worked for years and this company is bluffing more than you.

If, however, you find a big, fat, genuine Wurlitzer, in well-oiled working order and stuffed to the brim with recent singles owned by the company in question, you've struck pay dirt. Be extremely careful, this is bluff city – one false sneeze and the deal will be off and your career will be in tatters. When the man behind the desk gives you free access to his vaults to take away whatever CDs you desire, you will be tempted to conclude you are home and free. Wrong. Free CDs are the booby prize at this level.

The more experienced will have nipped round to the nearest pub, which will be littered with personnel from the major. Pick up a phone, preferably a mobile (though a TV remote will do), and feign a conversation in a loud voice: "Is that Steve Rival, Rival Records plc?" Go on to say that whilst you have the profoundest respect for him and his company, the £250,000 deal he has offered is not going to happen; then simply sit back, enjoy your drink, and wait.

Within seconds, you should be escorted back next door, past the mighty Wurlitzer, into the high speed lift, and ushered into the presence of the man nobody gets to meet – the managing director. The less you say, the better. Act dumb, drop the name of your lawyer if you have one, then leg it to your bus stop before you're rumbled.

c) **A huge bulbous juke box**, but alas, not a Wurlitzer. Be extremely cautious. This is the dreaded double bluff. Don't sign anything but listen extremely carefully to anything they have to say. They may be communicating a hidden message if you know how to interpret the clues "We could have bought a Wurlitzer but we're so successful we didn't need to". Then again, maybe not. If the offices look well upholstered and they appear to have staff, you might conceivably have lucked into a company that can actually help you to build a genuine career. More probably you've inadvertently banged your shin on the first rung of a slippery ladder, and will be sent back to Go without £200.

A&R

A&R, or 'Um and Err' as they are often called, stands for artist and repertoire, we think, but this fact can now be entirely forgotten, since no one can really remember why talent scouts are called A&R, but only that they are.

They are elusive creatures since they can never be found at their desks in the mornings (hangover time) and their afternoons consist of three-hour lunches and then a quick visit to several clubs to spot new up-and-coming talent. It is their job never to sign anyone while acting as though a new signing is imminent, and to convince everyone that they really do listen to each of the squillions of unsolicited demo tapes which record companies constantly receive. One office even kept a tea chest-full in reception, where every quivering wannabe couldn't help but see it on arrival, and have their insecurities further undermined.

With inverted pride, A&Rs can occasionally be heard quietly boasting that they "haven't signed anyone in two years". The discerning bluffer immediately knows this is code for "One more unsuccessful signing will mean the chop" so they daren't sign anything. This kind of paralysis is a recognised syndrome of A&R juniors and usually results in them finding promotion elsewhere as head of A&R, by which time they have long since learned that:

a) to trust their own feelings about what makes a record a hit is usually fatal
b) they should ignore what their ears tell them, keep quiet and leave judgement to others whose jobs are in less jeopardy (preferably the President).

The fact that no-one knows why some records are hits

and others are not is little consolation in a business where everyone has to pretend they do.

In any event, A&Rs do not actually sign anyone, they only make recommendations to the President, who then, if it's a UK President, flies off to America with a bag of cassettes to talk to his seniors there. The green light for a go project, that involves 'risk', i.e. money, more often than not will require a 'yes', from virtually everyone from the US President down to the local junior A&R. But it rarely involves the lost souls toiling in promotions, marketing, or sales because they actually have the best idea about what sells, what doesn't, and why. You figure it. One theory is that a record company promoter would say 'no' even to a platinum act, because less product and one good night's sleep are all they crave.

A&R are also meant to be the benign, friendly face suspicious artists can rely on to look after their interests in the company, as opposed to, say, the company's publicist, who may be sitting on the band's tour bus writing secret reports about the 'difficult' artist nearby and in particular, his private conversations and opinions about the record company. Should the artist find out about this CIA-style intrigue, and said artist has clout, i.e. sells millions of albums, expect a change of publicist at the next city truck stop, where they can also off-load the unwanted orange Smarties which were not on their rider. (See Glossary.)

One A&R man, from a well-respected label, having been suitably impressed by the artist performing in front of his eyes at a small club, turned to the artist's manager and said "He's fantastic, you should get my President down to see him". The next time you see ten empty seats in a prime spot at a concert, you will know that somewhere in the wings can be heard the howl of a manager who has spent five days setting up a perfect showcase gig to show off his artist in the best possible light only to have none of the A&R who promised to be there attend.

The recognised method to get A&R to your gig is to meet them at their office soon after they get back from lunch. Or, better still, meet them for lunch, keep them inebriated and amused all afternoon and, before they slip out again, take them with you to dinner and then on to the gig. Never allow an A&R man to promise you he will be there. His word in this regard is unfortunately worthless. If A&R attended every gig they promised to attend, they would have to be in ten places at once, though some nights the more conscientious may make it to four or five venues throughout the evening, the last one being something of a blur and therefore more likely to be reported back as a band not to be disregarded.

Marketing

Marketing people in the music business, like musicians, often suffer the same sense of not being in a 'proper' job, a job their Mum would have wanted for them. Pay will vary from nothing to lots, depending on the country and the status of the company. It is unlikely to correspond favourably to the amounts they would make selling shoes or computers in a 'real' company.

A marketing manager's expertise remains for the most part largely unused, but is put to best use when the time comes to move sales of a major artist from, say, five million to twenty million. Or to package a 'best of', or repackage old catalogue as yet another 'special' compilation – just what the world needs. More often he is dealing with the vagaries of the A&R's latest acquisition or, worse, his MD's latest 'discovery' (a Guatemalan flute player and his jazz-singing girlfriend found in a bistro on holiday), and the likely sales prospect of a few hundred units.

The marketing manager of a large record company is likely to be a fairly robust and versatile bluffer. He works in a business that reveals few solid trends and fewer clues as to what the public will decide they like next. Research is rarely undertaken and inevitably disregarded when it is. That the public is unpredictable is almost the only reliable predictor the marketing manager has.

When a new record is about to be released he will need to hold a meeting to rally his troops so they can listen to the record and organise a campaign. His budget is likely to be a quarter of what the artist's manager will expect, nay demand, and half of what he personally would prefer to have, and it will be three times what the company can realistically afford given the absence of research data to assist them in making rational decisions. His stall of goodies will in all probability be as cliché ridden as a gold Les Paul.

New records conform to the age-old maxim: 'A wheel is a wheel is a wheel; it cannot be reinvented three times a week'. So the promotion for the record will usually consist of the same elements each time, but in differing proportions, depending on budget, profile of the artist and the likelihood of success. These elements are Press, Radio and TV (please God), badges, stickers, posters, T-shirts, other promotional bribes and the one inoperable (but occasionally original) idea the artist wants his manager to instigate.

Like a politician, this bluffer will be adept at allowing everyone to hear what they want, while rearranging the same tired old clothes into the semblance of a new costume:

- bags instead of T-shirts
- smaller ads instead of ads
- Web sites instead of bright lights

Then his promotion team will be bullied, bribed, cajoled to get the thing loved (i.e. into the charts and selling).

You can always spot an inexperienced, or new, marketing manager by his insane willingness to put his head on the block and tell everyone which track in his expert judgement should be the first single from the new release, and how far up the charts it will go. Whereas the expert always has the perfect answer to hand. For example, if asked "How's the record/poster /T-Shirt, etc., coming along?" the answer will be carelessly thrown back, without choking, "FANTASTIC. Earth shattering. I've never seen a concept like it. It's going to be humungous." He'll never say "Have you got any paracetamol? I feel a migraine coming on". Whatever position is held in this business, a good bluffer never forgets that the only door truth opens is the exit to the job centre.

Promotions

To understand promotions, you need to know that the lives of those who work in this field revolve around one thing, apart from alcohol, and that is, the **charts**.

The important ones – the ones that make a difference financially – are the singles and albums charts. To join these holy listings, and see the chosen name rise higher each week, is to see that Dr. Pangloss was right and that indeed we do live in the best of all possible worlds. The great record-buying public in their wisdom have spoken. Fail to enter them and the experienced manager will apply the well-used, face-saving device that "It's all a lottery and a fix" – which usually falls on approving, sympathetic ears. If that doesn't work, declare that too much fame and exposure too quickly is a very bad thing. Say this enough times and you might even start to believe it.

Interviews

Every eager artist will do more interviews for radio, TV and the press than they have a snowflake's chance of remembering. Never admit to not remembering the interviewer the next time you inevitably meet them. The best tactic is to greet every interviewer like a long-lost comrade-in-arms, whether you've met before or not. Then they will assume it is they who can't remember.

Don't bother with pre-recorded interviews. Unless the voice of God personally promises you a big hit, a pre-recorded interview will not be used. Nor will the soundbites where you thank with false enthusiasm the DJ (who has yet to give you one miserable play at 4.30 a.m.) for single-handedly making your single a No. 1. The fact that the record company have only pressed 200 for radio and therefore the public will never see a copy, so it could never be a hit anyway, is another can of worms and not something you should shout about too loudly while on the premises of Radio Z.E.R.O. Home of the Stars. Provided you live within a fifty metre radius of the hospital you can get great reception.

Television Interviews

The first visit to a TV studio is a pretty exciting experience. By the time you are re-visiting the same studio with a third platinum album under your belt, you run the risk of finding it as enlivening as a visit to the dentist.

Studio-speak:

"We want this to be really special" = "Don't take one look at the set and walk out."

"That was great" = "We only ever do one take and you weren't worth a second one anyway."

"We'll fix it after the run through" = "It's not my problem, pal, we're going out live = what are you going to do, stop miming and demand a monitor?"

"From this angle it'll look good" = "Keep that microphone three feet below your mouth. We want to see the talent not hear it."

"We're using extra lights" = "This is the same set we use for our 10.30 chat show and if you think we're changing one light for you, mate, think again."

A singer-songwriter once walked into a TV studio where he was about to perform. The place was unusually quiet. To his surprise, the atmosphere was perfect for once. Not the usual blitzkrieg of lights; just some very tasteful, low key, lighting and a beautifully lit stool. He sat on the stool and looked tentatively at the monitor. His face, half lit, half shadowed, looked really moody. Wow. Quality. For once a director who knew his work. The crew returned from their lunch break; the lighting technician casually picked up the stool, his stool – the one he had been standing on to adjust the lights, and then switched back on all 300 lights at the director's command ready for the first, sweaty, run through.

Press and Radio Interviews

"When you're hot you're hot, and when you're not you're not" says your plugger, trying unsuccessfully to sound sympathetic. This is no comfort to the artist on the chill outside, who desperately wants to be in the warm glow of the inside, but it is the unenviable mountain that has to be climbed and what this business is all about.

"Don't bullshit the bullshitters" said the veteran radio promoter to an ambitious artist who, at the time, was being slightly over-expansive about his questionable success, after a particularly liquid lunch. He had confused a No. 1 import dance chart success with a US No. 1. In fact, this kind of economising with the truth is precisely what happens, and the collusion, like Chinese whispers, to create a disingenuous CV, has a convenience of purpose for all – to minimise the failures and maximise success. The artist exaggerates to the manager, who exaggerates to the President, who exaggerates to marketing, who exaggerate to promotions, who exaggerate to the media. Like the lawyer who prefers his client not to tell him if he's guilty, before long the intrepid radio promoter is doing a sales job on a dead artist (who at his prime never made it past No. 132 even in a radio chart), now convinced, and therefore convincing, that the next tour, just around the corner, will see this gifted, young person at No. 1, for certain.

Press promotions can involve the same deceptions. Simply substitute the music director at the radio station for the editor of Rock Dork Monthly and you get the picture. Even though voice-mail jail is where more and more calls end up, both parties need each other for their mutual survival. This is why both editors and music directors make maximum use of the telephone's voice-mail service: it keeps the bribes and bullshit from drowning them.

The Radio Station Interview

The new artist on his first trip to a radio station is in for a few surprises and the DJ will miss no opportunity in this initiation to make it an interesting one.

Memo to: All Presenters
From: Head of Music

The presenter should greet and talk to artists in a quiet, pleasant, relaxed way off-mike – or prior to starting the interview (we don't want them running off just yet). It is more effective to turn into an insensitive sadist once you go on air and your victim cannot then escape without looking petulant.

Make sure that their mike is smaller and inferior and set at a lower level than yours. Ditto their chair. That way, they will know who is boss and your audience will hear how much better your speaking voice is than the stammering amateur you are interviewing. We don't want the audience thinking just anyone can talk on air.

During the interview, never remotely offer eye contact, or acknowledge their presence until you pounce, unexpectedly, with your first question. Coffee may well spill through their nostrils. The opportunities for fun are endless. Once they are gibbering and cowering, you will have achieved the desired effect of making yourself sound superior.

Surprise is your best weapon. Remember that the more brutally unsympathetic you are, the faster you will make your name, so make your first question the mortal blow. For example: "So are the stories we've heard about you true that you still…(pick their least favourite topic, or one they have already answered 6,000 times before)…beat up/take drugs/deviate sexually/hate another band member", etc. "So Paul, was it hard working with a genius like John? Do you think it's still true that he was the more talented partner in the relationship?" Asking artists why they left their previous job – especially if it is completely irrelevant because it was decades ago can usually rattle their cage pleasantly too.

Another useful gambit is to ensure that artists sit doing nothing in your studio. This enables you to demonstrate your prowess and control over all you survey. They need never know that you have little influence over what you say or play.

As you remove the cellophane from the artist's CD, rustle it brusquely against the microphone. Let your audience know what you're up to. Show contempt for it all over your face, while expressing to the mike great enthusiasm about the record you have patently never listened to, and whose title you should not pronounce correctly, or better yet, do not announce at all. That way the listeners will not know what to order from the record store and you will have the deep satisfaction of thwarting your opponent in his/her reason for being there. The record promoter will continue to be nice to you when they call next week with a fresh victim, so why worry?'

Old hands at interviews will affect not to notice any of these ploys, even less so when meeting the producer of the show or the music director at the station – the people with the power to play or not to play records. The music director of a powerful station could be picking scabs from his feet as he stirs your tea, but the record company promoter will smile and sit on his lap as if he's Father Christmas.

It is generally expected that you will criticise the music biz in interviews (particularly if you're under 25), and have a spirited bash at your record company who sign all your pay cheques. There's plenty of time when you are older to gush gratefully in your sleeve notes and credit those 'best friends' you never met.

Alternatively, affect a hazy rural indifference. If asked about the latest hot signing, talk about your vegetable garden. If further pressed, enthuse about how well your broad beans did this year.

In an industry where dead air is the greatest sin, talk and be entertaining, or shut up and listen, but do not talk and be boring, otherwise how will you be distinguishable from everyone else?

THE DEAL AND HOW TO SURVIVE IT

The deal, can, at times, seem to be the whole story, the key, the *raison d'être* for everything. It isn't, but don't try telling that to those who are desperate to make records and reach a wider audience. They will even sit through lectures on copyright and the law after skipping every lecture at school and college in the hope of meeting someone, anyone, with even a tenuous line to a record company.

Contracts

There are contracts and there are contracts – from the no advance, one-single-plus-options kind, to the mighty mega-million deals of the superstars. There are also various types: recording contracts, publishing contracts, management contracts, agency contracts. The aspiring star is required to have a modest grasp of the essential qualities of each, when to sign and when to seek advice or say no.

Increasingly the rock music business is being driven by agreements inspired by 'the American contract' which is long, complicated and obtuse. The more obtuse a company makes its standard agreements, the harder it is for the artist or the manager to get to grips with what the companies are really up to. The only people who understand them are company lawyers who have a fluid grasp of every sneaky sub-clause because they have spent all their lives incorporating one little trap after another. Their positions remain apparently unassailable. However, the quality of their signings aren't, since only those artists with the patience of Job, or nowhere else to go, would stick around nine months waiting for a deal to complete, while their work becomes stale.

The best deals are resolved in a matter of days, or at any rate not months, and if you have to have more than two meetings about it, nothing very good is likely to result – with the proviso that you do not forget that the best deal will still be the best one you can get.

Recording Contracts

This is normally the deal between the recording artist and his or her future record company. Without the deal, artists can make recordings to their heart's content, assuming they have money to burn, but they won't have a commercial conduit for exploiting them. If artists allow their manager to negotiate it for them, certain distinct advantages to the manager will accrue. If the artists allow their own lawyer to negotiate it, then certain large bills will accrue. It's a Hobson's choice for a young, hungry band.

The best deal will depend entirely upon the perceived value of the product, which normally means the artist. If the artist has a six page spread in this month's fashionable music mag – hold on to your hats – the price is going up. Try getting six pages after the deal is signed and it will, in all probability, cost the company's entire advertising budget for a year. It is a frequent practice to trade off, quid pro quo, interview space supplied by the magazine editors in return for advertisements being placed by the record company. But expect every editor to tell you that while he or she would never trade their integrity for mere advertising revenue, they know plenty of others who would.

A regular recording contract will contain the same few standard clauses, but each will vary, in terms of amounts and percentages, depending on the relative bargaining positions of the players.

One would normally expect to see the following:

Term: This should be straightforward but isn't. It is meant to be the length of time the artist and his/her work is under contract to the company. Four years, for example, would not be unusual. Thereafter artists might reasonably hope to be either staying with the label and therefore extending the deal, or leaving the label, with all the product in their own possession. That this rarely happens is because the record company would prefer to hold on to the rights, forever if possible, even after they no longer have any interest in the artist. This way they can horse-trade at a later date if the artist despite all odds enjoys success elsewhere. The last thing you want, if you're a record company man, is an artist leaving your label and then achieving great success with someone else. You want all your ex-artists to remain buried, otherwise you run the risk of looking as if you didn't know what you were up to when you dropped them.

Territory: This is the geographical area within which the record company plan to control and exploit the product being offered to them. It may be only two or three countries such as GAS (Germany/Austria/Switzerland) or it may be a deal for the World, which usually contains pretentious clauses about the universe – to protect future income from aliens presumably.

Similarly, defining 'a record' as 'a carrier of sound, including CD, digital and audio cassette and of any format yet to be invented' is a typical way a record company will try to ensure that, when a new format does come along, like MP3, they have retained the right to ex-ploit it at preferential rates. If they fail to get this clause incorporated, any good manager will immediately use a new format as an opportunity to re-negotiate the contract.

Renegotiation these days, under any pretext, is becoming almost as prevalent, and necessary, as the signing itself. A shameless device used by less scrupulous record companies is to sign for the world when they only have a distribution network big enough to exploit inner London. Equally, a European signing of, say, Norwegian Fjord Folk Singers of the 14th Century though signed for the world including satellite and Internet rights, doesn't necessarily imply that it will be exploited (i.e. sold) in your local Virgin megastore.

Advances: This is the amount of non-repayable cash that the company will pay to the artist for each record delivered. Typically, the record company will offer huge amounts on later hypothetical albums, but as little as possible on album 1, confident that they alone will have an option to continue or terminate the deal when it suits them.

The best deal from the artist's point of view may be the one where the record company commits, without options, to more than one album. Equally, if the band is already selling millions of albums, it may well be more interested in the size of the royalty since it can assume (unless the advance was gargantuan) that it will recoup its advance anyway. The higher the royalty, the sooner the recoupment is complete, and the sooner the companies have to make ongoing payments every few months. Large record companies hire financial controllers just to play around with this

32

cash flow creatively. Even Stars and those representing them may employ similar uneven-handedness with former band members' assets, especially those without ongoing solo value to their record company.

Financial controllers keep the company's stock options healthy. It is their job to make the company's accounts look as bad as possible in year one of their tenure (the fault of their predecessors), to make the company look as good as possible in year two (their personal triumph), and to be into a new job and gone in year three, before the accounts are published. A&R personnel may practise a similar technique by signing acts at insanely inflated prices, only to be promoted to the rival firm before anyone finds out that, despite gold discs and sales in excess of a million for the artist signed, the company still makes a whacking loss.

Royalties and Deductions: This is the percentage per record payable to the recording artist. Thus if a record were retailing at, say, £10, a deal offering 15% of retail would pay the artist £1.50 on each record sold...if pigs flew. In reality, the record companies have more ways than anyone can list to ensure that this simply doesn't happen. Here are just a few of their better known 'economies':

1. They pay on dealer (wholesale), not retail, price.
2. They pay on what they call dealer price, but in fact it is set much lower.
3. They reduce the royalty by anything between 10-25% for packaging. This is based on the old notion that recordings made at 78 rpm broke frequently in transit to retailers, but it is a clause vigorously defended to this day.
4. They pay royalties on CDs, as if they were still selling LPs.

5. They try to deduct as many of their promotional expenses against the artist's share of royalty as possible. For example, if they have a clause saying that a TV media campaign will result in half royalties, then they can place a couple of cheap ads on cable and say that all royalties for a certain period must be 'capped'.

The ingenuity of both companies and managers to find new ways to increase their share would appear limitless. It is not unheard of for a manager to secure for his band large sums of money from the record company (say 50% recoupable against royalties) for tour support and then proceed to give the record company a set of highly inflated costings, only to pocket the difference.

How much the manager gets will depend on the artist/manager contract which is another minefield. Unscrupulous managers have been known to do deals with concert promoters in which not only their artist but the inland revenue are soundly trounced: the listed fee payable to the artist will appear unbelievably modest but a large unlisted balance arrives, in brown envelopes, on the manager's desk some days later.

Most recording deals divide neatly into three types:

1. **Take-the-money-and-run deals** – sometimes known as 'coach and horse' deals (a deal so flabby you could drive a coach and horses through it). Here you maximise the advance, minimise the term, create innumerable ambiguous clauses and hope to get out of it as soon as possible – after one or two albums would be ideal – hopefully with your back catalogue in tow. Only recommended for terminal rock stars.

2. **Good deals** – ones where you believe the company
   has the necessary vision and ability to build your
   profile. Here you maximise royalties, maximise the
   length of their commitment, maximise their promotional obligations, generally all face the same
   direction and invest in your future. This is the best
   deal possible until the person who signed you
   leaves for a rival company. Then it's the worst.
   People who work for companies are rarely influ-
   enced by what is best for the company unless it also
   happens to be what is best for them. Certainly there
   is no point in making the particular company you
   work for rich if you aren't going to get all the glory,
   the pay rise and the promotion. Any manager
   hoping to get anywhere with the majors needs to
   understand this awkward truth as his first base.

3. **The deal you shouldn't do.** This is the deal most
   artists sign up for as the Faustian price of admis-
   sion to the party.

Lawyers

As a bluffer, all you have to remember is that in the
music business solicitors are called lawyers and that
a number of them will charge like rhinos unless you
tie them down to a sensible price before you start.

Financial Advisers

In terms of glamour (rather than wealth), financial
advisers are often the poor relations of the music business, as lowly in status as those who work for collection agencies, unless they rise to become Presidents,
when they become feared and loathed for their per-

ceived absence of credibility. "No ears" is an oft-whispered back stab for these corporate success stories, meaning they succeeded by being good at making money for the company, rather than at understanding artists' foibles and their music. This is the great divide in the rock business and it is a wise executive who avoids being tagged too heavily in either camp.

Accountants

The perceived objective of an accountant who looks after the finances of recording artists is to convince them to have as many companies as possible – each one of which will require lucrative maintenance for many years to come – and to invest as much of their profits as possible in pension schemes run by a broker who preferably splits his commission with the accountant.

As long as they prevent the tax authorities from arresting the artist for non payment, busy musicians are usually so grateful, despite the inordinately high fees, and anyway so baffled and bewildered by figures, that they wilfully leave the 'money stuff' to the accountants to get on with. For obvious reasons many managers would prefer to see their artists use the same accountants as they do, and their lawyers too, if they think they can get away with it. But a Chinese wall is never as reliable as a different street altogether.

As an artist you will inevitably be led towards allowing your manager and accountant access to controlling aspects of your finances to a degree that they themselves would never allow anyone to have on their own finances. Be aware and, like good government, try to keep each branch independent of the other. You'll fail, but it will be a valiant effort.

Pensions

By all means have a pension – but, don't have more than one or, at a pinch, two, especially if your affairs were already strategically and hopelessly out of control before you found financial enlightenment. Seven schemes, whilst brilliantly lucrative for your numerous advisers, are simply too onerous to support, especially if your friendly broker has explained the benefits of front-loading your pension with a massive, ongoing, yearly commitment.

Remember that when they say "You don't need to make these payments each year", this is likely to be a bluff too ignoble for words. It is true that you don't need to make annual payments, but if you don't, perhaps your pension will be worth less than the figure you first put in? Pay the taxes and keep your commitments small at first. You can always elect to add additional sums at your own volition as time goes on. Your accountant is there to help you through this, and you can obtain a particularly altruistic one c/o the fairies at the bottom of the garden.

It could be a good idea to pre-empt difficulties and announce to prospective 'advisers' that your father/wife/brother/sister is a renowned pensions' expert. The sharks will go and circle elsewhere; then you can choose an uncomplicated, commission-free, ethical scheme off the shelf.

If the scheme performed in the top quarter say for the last seven years, it will probably be okay for another seven. It's another 'nobody knows anything' scenario so you can be reasonably confident of one thing: that the last person who will really know what's in your best interest is the one who claims to do so.

MAKING A RECORDING

Once you have signed your deal, or even induced some A&R interest in getting you a deal, you will need to venture into a studio. This is such a breath of fresh air, compared to the horror of the money machine, that some people spend their entire lives in womb-like darkness, never seeing daylight at all.

Studios

A commercial recording studio can cost anything from a few tens of thousands of pounds, to many millions, to create. There is little relationship between the cost of a studio and its ability to generate hits – other than the fact that hit acts use expensive studios, so expensive studios have more hits.

Real World Studio, Peter Gabriel's multi-million pound playground in Bath, was celebrated when it was first built as being pretty special, which it is, but Gabriel himself records in an inspiringly idiosyncratic way that makes little direct use of the extraordinary technology available. It's not unusual for dance hits to originate in a teenage bedroom with just a keyboard, a couple of boxes and a computer for company. A correlation between equipment and commercial results would therefore appear questionable.

However, what working in a hit-making studio does do is give you a feeling of confidence and incentives to match, or attempt to better, the quality of other comparable artists. It's a blast to work where your heroes have gone before.

Equipment

The first thing to realise about equipment is that the rock music market is not driven by science or facts, it's driven by irrational feelings, hormones and tittle-tattle. Certain bits of equipment get a reputation and become sacred items that no-one dares criticise – though criticism is fierce and furious in this area of the business.

What every studio has at its heart, apart from an overdraft with the bank, is a recording console – also known as 'the desk' – a monster with millions of knobs. The seasoned bluffer knows how to dodge this issue. Explain with great gravitas to the sound engineers that you're not the 'hands on' kind and that you respect their right to make their contribution (i.e. twiddle the knobs without interference). Many well-respected artists and producers have got away with this useful ruse. In fact, if you know how to change the bass and treble on your hi-fi then you are well on your way to understanding what this thing actually does.

A veteran explained it thus: "Call your sound signal Mr Signal. Mr Signal leaves your guitar and goes to the desk. Mr Signal then whizzes around inside the circuitry of the desk, generating reverbs, delays, more signal noise, less middle, etc. He gets temporarily lost until someone figures out how to get him to a tape machine and back to the desk which he just left, so you can now actually hear it." By then it will normally sound considerably worse than it did when you first played a note. This is because the longer the time spent getting your sound just right, the more money the studio will make.

In the process of recording, headphones are commonplace, and a number of misunderstandings between the control room (the one with the desk in it) where the engineer and producer normally sit and the live room (with the live performers) are inevitable – "I said phase it, not erase it". It helps to have visual contact between the rooms (usually soundproofed glass) so that, for example, when the singer makes a circular hand gesture a game of charades can ensue: "I know; it's a crashing helicopter. No, it's got lots of wheels. Oh... rewind the tape. Why didn't you say so?"

Expect to hear mutterings about '3k' (the frequency up around the vocal where everything wants to compete for space), and '50 hertz' (the frequency down below the bass guitar which induces a sensation of temporary incontinence). If you want to pretend you've got better hearing than a dog, talking about 16k will make you the envy of every cutting engineer, but be prepared for the term 'wanker' to follow you as you pass the musicians on their cigarette break.

You should know that Neve consols are warm, that SSLs are good for mixing but a bit too clinical to record with unless customised, that pre-CBS fenders are classic and that valve mikes, especially old Neumans, should be worshipped from afar and are only brought out of storage for singers who are members of the inner circle of the cognoscenti. Ancient valve microphones look the best but usually hum and rumble to the point where this can't disguise the fact that they're basically museum pieces and not half as good as the new ones.

One gifted guitarist once remarked that he always chose his guitars for how they looked because "You'll always play better if you look cool." This is not a bad starting point for understanding equipment and the music biz. Woe betide the studio that buys a million quid's worth of perfect gear, only to find that the 19 year-old lead singer from this week's platinum No. 1. band prefers to use something his hero used twenty years earlier.

Generally be ready to have a flexible combination of the latest toys and some shagged-out old dross. Gear is sexy. You'll quickly become an addict and need to be updating constantly. Blink, and what you already possess will be derided as clichéd, and the new bigger, faster, better (i.e. incompatible) upgrade will already be upon you. It can bankrupt even the most robust star faster than a gifted pensions adviser.

Producers

If you know the names of any three albums which have sold over twenty million copies, then simply to name the credited producers of these albums as firm favourites will leave the profundity of your wisdom pretty much beyond question.

You should probably also know the 'A List' of truly talented producers. Trevor Horn, for example, has held a seat akin to that of a godhead, with Daniel Lanois a close second. Then there are the ones whose moves are invisible – the 'we don't need to be there' school – who don't, to the uninitiated, seem to do much or even be present when the record is being made, but as if by magic keep reappearing in the Top Ten.

Ignorance is bliss, and many blissfully rich producers know this to be true. A word of caution, however. Because producing is a job that seems to the untrained eye to be simple, it beckons to more rock bluffers than most other professions in the business. Many avid engineers and musicians want 'to be the boss' for a while, perceiving that the best thing about the job is that producers do not have to support the records they make by undergoing tours, but receive a share of the royalties anyway. (They are unaware that there are countless producers still waiting for theirs.)

The best producers get to work on the best records, but are only as good as the song, the session players, the record company executive and his budget allow them to be – not forgetting the artists, of course – the most common mistake young producers make.

It's no use making a wonderful backing track only to find that it's in a useless key for the singer, or that the track is too huge to fit the frail voice over it. To quote a Neil Young song, "What we've got here" (says the producer), "is a perfect track, but we don't have a singer and we don't have a song." Start with the singer.

The more people you can keep away, the easier your job will be, which is the reason everybody gives for recording in Montserrat or Compass Point. You may even be believed, provided you invite the A&R man along for the ride.

Producers have a number of ploys to tyrannise the artist or experienced session musician (i.e. one who not only plays really well, but knows more about production than the producer). One is to regularly halt the proceedings, just when everyone is starting to enjoy themselves, and say that they think the timing was off – then make them do it again without checking. If the band are sufficiently new to wear it, such a Producer might last through the project until mature enough to go to the bathroom unaided.

Session Musicians

According to a famous session bass player (call him PP) the session musician's career has four stages. Stage one: Who's PP? Stage Two: Get me PP. Stage Three: Get me a young PP. Stage Four: Who's PP?

One aggrieved session musician turned to the manager of a famously difficult artist and said, "I've got four rates I charge for my playing and they all get you the same quality. They are: Mates Rate, Cheap rate, Expensive Rate, and your F**&ng artist's rate." The price may vary from negligible pay with a nice meal and drinks thrown in, plus petrol, to thousands per day, where the first five days consist of tuning up the drum kit. Experienced producers recognise that if they've got a reasonable budget and don't want to waste time auditioning, it's almost always cheaper to use someone fast and reliable, even if expensive. Better to record a part in two hours for £200, than a part in five hours for £50, especially if you're paying £100 per hour for the studio.

Sound Engineers

These are the ones who twiddle all the buttons, are mercifully devoid of any wish to make an 'artistic' judgement, leave their personality at home, and have no sex life because they suffer terminal sleep deprivation.

Here are a few common expressions heard by the engineers over the talkback and what they really mean:

Producer to Musicians:
"That was really good" = Let's just do one more.
"Let's do one more" = We're going to be here until I

say you're finished.

"We'll fix it in the mix" = Your performance isn't worth saving: we'll have to lose it.

"That was great" = That take might just be worth playing back to see it it's worth trying to repair.

"It'll save time" = It'll take longer, but I want to do it my way.

Artist to Producer:

"I've got a terrible headphone balance' = I've just made another blunder so we'll have to do another take.

"That's interesting" = That would be interesting on someone else's record, not mine.

"It'll save time" = It'll take longer but I want to do it my way.

Promo Videos

Exhibitionism dovetails perfectly into the main artery of a rock star's vanity. Every self-adoring rock-god intuits very quickly that hit acts are always on television, ergo hit acts have videos, ergo make a video and be a hit act. Alas, not so. Videos get made in something approaching the same proportion as recording artists make CD albums – which means that the vast majority hit the morgue slabs only minutes after arriving from the on line editing room to the record company.

Artists like to feel they have some artistic control in the creation of the visual story that will accompany their single. The industry's pose is to let them find a video they already like, and thereby a style they like, and then try to find a production company for them willing to attempt a similar job (for much less money) while all the while convincing them that Betacam rather than 35ml is costing much more.

If the artist is a major star, expect the company to spend infinitely more than even the chosen director ever dreamt possible for four minutes of footage. A cast of thousands, well known actors, extravagant film sets and computerised virtual reality special effects will be prerequisites. This will soon quadruple any projected budget. The star has artistically climaxed when the finished result looks stiff, derivative, dishonest and somehow amateur. It will then undoubtedly be popularly taken up by all and sundry.

There are two types of video director:

1. Those who want to make movies and therefore see the video as a showcase for their directorial debut. Since these are usually newcomers, you can safely recognise them because the less they know, the more they will boss everyone else about and generally make sure that attention is focussed on themselves.

2. Those who make tasteful, interesting videos that are enormously admired by the producer and the video company secretary. Only use this type if you want to make ambient arthouse music for your friends, or if you are so successful you can afford to risk 'Art'. The perfect example of making use of fame to go arthouse was director Steven Spielberg. Rock examples also exist but are somewhat less lofty – George Michael from Wham to, well... George Michael.

Videos get made because there is a one in a hundred chance it might actually get played a lot and thereby produce a hit. As the principal outlets for video are specialist TV channels like MTV and VH1, it is often argued (by those who have to pay for them to be made) that neither counts for anything like as many consequent sales as a performance on a top-rated, syndicated chat show, like David Letterman. So unless your last album went Gold in a half dozen territories, expect some resistance from your record company when you ask for fifty grand to make one.

If you are a struggling artist with no budget and little company support, you could consider becoming an auteur for a month. But do-it-yourself (directing, telecineing, editing, producing) is so fraught with unforeseeable difficulties that no amount of bluffing will help. It can be done, but not if you want to sleep, or keep all your marbles, and certainly not if the record is already charting and you need a promo video by this time next week. A production house may cost more, but you will still have the hair and friends you started out with.

TOURING

This is the real dynamo – the engine room – of the business. All the best and worst aspects of rock 'n roll are to be found on tour. It is where the crack and sizzle of charisma is put to the test, and where reason and sanity are left behind. You can put Franken-stein's monster – bolts and all – on stage and hear two vacant girls in the front row make the following exchange: "What do you think of the large guy?" "Hmm...really cute in a rugged kind of way."

Frankenstein's homemade daughter would receive no less reverence, because the issue is not about gender, it's about the fame and celebrity that a stage engenders like no other. Though touring is the most exhausting thing imaginable, some people take to it like junkies to their fix. More usually you will find each day leading up to show-time akin to having your personality slip away from you, like watery jelly through a sieve, with the psychoses this induces becoming damaging to the point of drug abuse, alcoholism and/or therapy, whichever presents first. Paradoxically you can go to bed each night confident that you have had an enduring experience you will be certain never to remember.

In this scenario the recording artist, who is often the song-writer too, begins to suffer mild feelings of schizophrenia which can start as early as first rehearsals. Problem one. You still feel like you're a musician and part of the gang. Wrong. You are the musos' employer now, and they will hit you for the bill every time they need their free T-shirts washed and stage suits dry cleaned. They will get irritable with you for suckering them into this tour if the gigs aren't sell-outs or the promoter thinks a urinal is the right place to leave your burgers when the rider says you're vegetarian. Hey it's show business, what do you want? Look good and never mind the sweat marks on yesterday's dress shirt.

Take heart. There is a touring law which says, that the better things get, the more musicians complain. It's one way of passing time when 90% of their time consists of being locked up in transportation instead of playing music, which after all is the only thing they know to do to stop themselves becoming as hopelessly dysfunctional as they really are.

Agents and Concert Promoters

To organise a series of concerts, a rock group will first need to employ the services of an agent. The agent will charge 10% (normally) of the advance fee paid by the concert promoters in each country the group is proposing to visit. The concert promoter will therefore need to front (i.e. gamble) large sums of money.

Concert promoters are a much maligned and misunderstood species in this business. These days we know gambling to be a sickness, so a more sympathetic treatment of them by the agent might be expected. Concert promoters will attempt to offset their costs to the agent by getting each venue, or each local promoter, to front up as much as possible of the total fee they will need to hand over to the Agent, who in turn will pass it on to the band's manager (less commission).

As with recording contracts, there are no fixed rules, but here is a not untypical scenario. A young Welsh folk singer, Morgan, the church organ player, much to everyone's surprise not least himself, has a huge mainstream, global hit. 'I'm Just a Lonesome Whinger', along with the existential angst of its B side 'Flowers are Pretty', goes top ten everywhere. Comparisons with weighty rivals make front-page stories in the rock press. Morgan with his organ has crossed over: he has gone from being a folk-cult, of interest only to a minority of specialists and fans, to being supermarket-famous overnight. There is an immediate scramble to get this artist out on the road.

The newly acquired manager phones an agent. The agent phones concert promoters all over the world and a tour begins to be assembled.

Because it depends upon availability, the venues provided for this fee do not make much sense acoustically or geographically. The band is sent scuttling backwards and forwards, like a crazed roadrunner, criss-crossing the same autobahns and motorways endlessly (or until they can afford to fly).

Crews

These are the extras, the characters who, in the cinema, suffer the fate of their namesgoingpastsofast on the credits, that not even Superman could read them. A band, when touring, will take with them anything from one sound engineer (sound of mind and body anyway), to 200 crew.

The budget and perceived requirements never tally. Some hard rock bands regard a roadie who can make a good cup of tea at soundcheck in, say, Baden-Baden, more important than their singer, others place a higher premium on a lighting designer. It's a matter of personal taste, but the size of venue and the expected audience are, in professional terms, the basis upon which soberish judgements are likely to be made. That no-one knows what number will (or won't) turn up until the night is par for the rock 'n roll course.

"Someone should've said no" is commonly heard by exhausted crew (and band) on tours when the distances between gigs become prohibitive. There's a good reason why no-one ever does say 'no' and that is money. With overheads rising in excess of £300,000 per night, which for huge rock venues with massive stages and security can easily happen, you don't want too many nights off – especially when the gross take is likely to be more than a million pounds (a mere 60,000 punters at twenty quid a ticket, for instance). The fact that the monitoring engineer fancies a night off in Amsterdam to visit an old girlfriend cannot justify losses of hundreds of thousands of dollars which a single night not generating income could represent.

Each tour a band completes, like soldiers completing a tour of duty, creates solidarity and other ritual bondings as they climb the slippery slope of success. As budgets increase and crews become larger, pressure groups and lobbies evolve to press management for the items they absolutely need (i.e. would like to have), on tour. The crew will want inexhaustible supplies of equipment. The band want inexhaustible supplies of crew.

Imagine a huge travelling circus, but with more electrical gear than you could fit into a large Superstore. The number of articulated lorries on the road for a tour can be a matter of considerable prestige. Only six artics, and your cachet may be seen to be falling. It's a dilemma for the image-conscious. Order more lights and bass bins – even if the crew never unload them? No, the manager calls a press conference (which in reality may only be an assembly of five adolescents from the various fanzines) and announces that you have no less than three separate crews, busy leap-frogging each other across the world, so lavish is the scale of the entertainment you will be providing. That way, even if they count your trucks, and they're not likely to be the world's most numerate, they'll figure – six times three – "Wow, that's six, er, six times three, er, lots of trucks" and be suitably impressed.

If the musicians are by this stage chemically challenged (which they may well be if they've been worked to death for the last 18 months), so rarely do bands and crew get together, the manager could tell them the same guff and retire on the proceeds.

The crew boss is likely to want to see that his crew and himself have things like:

- a day off once in a while
- a high quality crew bus with beds
- a hot meal at every venue
- shortish travelling times so that after they dismantle the stage they can get some sleep before setting it up somewhere else.

The band will want:

- a rider which provides for macrobiotic diets
- personal roadies (a guitar roadie or two for the guitarist, a drum roadie for the drummer)
- opportunities for prayer, meditation, use of a gym, voice and body massage...
- a girlfriend who insists on flying out for the Milan gig. She'll need a ticket and a limo.

The possibilities are fairly limitless, and include anything which recording artists think they will need to help them feel good on the night. Since ultimately the whole show depends upon this, even the most eccentric requests are usually acceded to.

When it comes to equipment, bands normally like volume – in both senses of the word – but crews, who on occasion may not have humpers to assist them in carrying the gear in and out, are more prone to measure their status by the quality, rather than volume, of what they carry. It's easier to sound like a sound engineer who knows what he's doing if you've been supplied with equipment that you know will deliver a hi-fi performance, even if it ripped a hole in the budget the size of the missing ozone over the north pole. Similarly a lighting technician will go on opting for more lights until the national grid curls up and dies, even if most of the time he's saving them for the big finale.

Expect a conversation between two sound engineers to go something like this:

"So what have you been doing?"

"Oh I went out with Jessie James last month. We went down a storm."

"I've heard she's really difficult."

"Yeah well, it's her call. She pays the bills. I just mix her vocal too loud so she loves me. We're off to Asia next week."

"Lucky bastard."

"No, I'm on monitors" (sympathetic sounds from his colleague). "But I did the out front sound for the Pope in Jerusalem at the weekend. That was a blast. You should've been there. Yo. Cities – wreck 'em and leave 'em."

The Hotel

For the promoter, a good hotel is a cheap hotel, provided the artist or the band will put up with it without becoming 'difficult'. However the band will, in all probability, want to see real swans swimming in the foyer and champagne cocktails at check in, not because of the swans, but because it will indicate positive proof that:

– the towels will be large, white, plentiful and fluffy-clean
– the phones will work
– there will be 24 hour room service, even if the street noise during the night is so loud that a brandy coma can't obliterate it.

Years of running on empty, shivering with a small, damp, worn-out towel after a feeble shower, in a tired, depressing room, and not getting messages about soundcheck being two hours late, have taught them the hard way that good hotels are not a luxury but one of the many crucial aides to survival on the gruelling training course called touring.

Even the elephant-killing shots of adrenalin generated by the performance on the night, simply aren't enough to carry most people through the whole experience without a secure and comfortable place to collapse in (and party in) afterwards.

The crazed spirit of this high-on-fatigue paradox is a recognised syndrome and an accepted part of the package. On U2's 'End of the World' tour the production co-ordinator at an airport waiting for an all night flight to Tokyo surveyed the assembled wreckage of musicians and others and said, "If we took all the broken parts here and put them together we might get one human being."

Time is the great enemy on tour: for the artist it's the time spent doing nothing; for the crew it's the opposite. They have an impossible regime – getting all the gear assembled in time for soundcheck late afternoon, through to disassembling and moving it on to the next venue – a relentless 24-hour rota which leaves little room for 'oversights' on the part of the local promoter, the one who is supposed to ensure that the myriad essential things requested have, in fact, been provided even if, in the event, no-one touches them.

The Tour Manager

This is the person who travels with the band, looks after their needs, liaises with the crew, collects the cash from the promoter and does the accounts at 3 a.m., after phoning the manager in his home time zone: in effect, a manager 'in absentia' for the road.

It's 10.35 a.m. The tour manager has just missed breakfast (again) and the bus out front is ready to leave. Everyone is in it, except one rigger, who is not answering his phone. He was last seen amorously absorbed the night before with a scantily clad fan from the front row. The same one with a passing fancy for Frankenstein's monster. Once the rigger's bedroom door has been opened, and the gaffer tape removed from his wrists, he is as good as new.

Many rock bands after doing their stadium gig will retire to a small jazz club to blow away the tensions of the over-rehearsed theatrical show by indulging in some spontaneous musicianship and enjoying a more intimate contact with their audience. To be seen by an audience at the back of a 50,000 seat auditorium, gestures from the stage need to be choreographed and larger than life. With 200 lights shining in your face you are staring into black – with the nearest face at least 15 meters away, and that's just the drummer. You are not going to get any precise sense about your audience. Are they smiling/snoozing/burping/waving/jeering/dancing? In a small club your front row will be three feet away and you will see and hear everyone in the room. The feedback will be immediate and very direct. A London club will be characterised by an expression of deep affection, "Get on with it, you C*@t."

Just as no recording artist escapes financially without getting burned by an operator, no-one escapes long-term rock touring physically or emotionally unburned either:

Wasted guitarist: "This stage looks familiar."

Promoter: "It should do, you played it six months ago."

HOW TO WRITE

a) Dance Music

A successful young dance record producer was explaining to a failed middle-aged bass player why he had just been given an advance of £300,000 by a music publisher. Intrigued, the old deaf rocker asked how a veteran trouper like himself might go about having a dance hit and was told: "Tune to Radio One for about thirty seconds, copy the drum pattern, loop it. Play one chord over it incessantly. Then get someone famous, ethnic or cute, or better yet all three, to yell banal clichés over it."

b) Mainstream American Rock

Give yourself a name that doesn't appear to mean much – Bon Jovi, for example. Make sure your singer looks cute, then try to sound exactly like Bruce Springsteen. Only stop doing this when successful enough to be regarded as the source of rather than successor to the style.

c) Country Music

Be born singing on a horse. Be seen to live in Nashville. Have a Stars and Stripes or, better yet, Confederate flag, flying over your house. Drive a huge customised truck to the supermarket. Keep the structures of your tunes simple, which any songwriter will tell you is actually devilishly complicated, and sing about trite everyday things like love, or travelling the US. Tell it in a uniquely derivative way, then find your gorilla, i.e. cultivate a relationship with successful recording artists and convince them that you wrote this song with each of them in mind. After fifty tries, you might get one dumb enough to believe you and cover your song. Don't wait for any publisher to do it for you – they're much too busy counting all the money being made from other writers.

d) Your Own Songs

Even if you start out as purely derivative, to be a singer-songwriter you will need to suffer some serious slings and arrows and generally walk your own lonely road with only a sack of cold Russian cabbage for company, to find your authentic voice. This is not a voyage on which to embark if the jet-setting high-life appeals.

You will need to make a fleet of uncommercial albums and if possible have a couple of books under your belt around the time of your mid-life crisis. Painting the odd canvas as a sideline is fine (Joni Mitchell does it, after all), but doesn't in itself demonstrate quite enough corroborative evidence of suffering and angst.

Ideally, try to have a best selling album somewhere around No. 3 or 4, and then become obscure and reclusive until your new records and your numerous bootlegs appear indistinguishable. You should admire Bob Dylan's 'Blonde on Blonde' or 'Highway 61 Revisited', but only if you're ready to field a fleet a questions from an enthusiast. Van Morrison's 'Astral Weeks' never fails to work.

You should try to have hitchhiked the world, known John Lee Hooker or Muddy Waters; have slept with Jack Kerouac (it's okay, he's dead, though they may cotton on if you were born in the last couple of decades); had conversations with famous jazz players and be suitably reverential about dead artists, especially if they died poor.

In the early years, write about the perfidy of love, dead end jobs and your impending psychoses; in the later ones, the struggle with God and the venality of the entrenched powers-that-be, particularly their indifference to the work of great artists, i.e. you.

MUSIC PUBLISHERS

To the record company, the publisher is a waste of space, useful only for the pittance they contribute towards promotions. To the publisher, the record companies are manned by people with cloth ears. To the artist, unless these people understand what Jesus and Van Gogh suffered, then a plague on both their houses. Only the manager, the polecat politician, can effectively straddle all these contradictory worlds, agreeing with everyone's viewpoint while keeping a clear hand on the tiller and the winning post (his off-shore bank account) firmly in sight.

So what do music publishers do? This oft-asked question is one to which few have discovered a satisfactory answer. They do what the collection agencies do – they have lots of money and therefore need to celebrate a lot. They also do one other vital thing: they pay advances. When you've made your record, they know that mechanicals should flow, or at least trickle, from the record company to the collection agencies to themselves. They also know that performance royalties will follow if the record gets played, particularly on radio. So, like bookies, they work out the odds and pay accordingly, and take a percentage of what the agencies pay (anywhere between 10% to 50%) for doing so.

A standard (nothing is ever standard in this business) 75/25 writer/publisher split would mean that after the radio station pays out its spondoolies for what it has logged (for playing, say, Jed Spogg's hit CD 'Too Chunky for My Jeans') and the collection agencies have taken their share, the rest goes to Jed's publisher who takes 25% of what it receives and passes the remainder to its financial controller who holds on to it, until writs fly, and then uses it to pay off the advances the publisher has paid to the manager.

The manager takes his commission from what he receives, and anything else he can write off to expenses or lose in the shuffle, then passes the rest to the accountants (whom you may recall, may or may not be the manager's accountants). The accountants take what they feel they are entitled to, pay the inland revenue, the customs and excise and the pensions advisers (split commissions thank you), then pass the remaining amount to the artist's financial advisers. The financial advisers take what they feel they are entitled to and pass what is left to the artist's bank manager. The bank deducts its usual charges plus a small consultancy for the bridging loan secured by the accountants, and the overdraft goes to the divorce attorneys.

We think this is fairly typical, but by all means write your own version if you're not satisfied.

GLOSSARY

The Act – The band, the artist, anyone who performs on a stage. In the context of the music business, normally a musical act.

AOR – Adult Orientated Rock, format abbreviation introduced like so many (AAA, etc.), by American radio. If floundering, invent your own three letters and quote from a non-existent magazine, say, Insiders Rock Riders Radio Weekly.

A&R – Talent scouts who don't actually ever sign anyone.

Artists – The talent, or those who perform.

The Boss – Bruce Springsteen.

Dead Heads – People with dead heads, we think. Oh, hang on a minute, memory loss is a terrible thing and has, we believe, something to do with the marijuana plant, but we can't quite make the synaptic connection. Mrs Flittersnoop, our Lady that dies, we mean does, says they are fans of a group called The Grateful Dead fronted by a dead person called Jerry.

DJ – Someone with a name like a student entertainments rep (e.g. Dave Spart) who punts records to punters. Very few still choose their own records; they rely on producers to do that for them.

Dressing room – Tatty, depressing place which often doubles as the W.C., where bands fight with each other in private, then party in and trash, after the gig.

Fame spotters – Those who love autographs like regular fans love music.

Fans – a) Those who very much like the work of a particular artist; b) those who artists wave to from the safety of their tour bus/stage/limo.

Feedback – Unintentional audio loop, great for clearing a control room of unwanted guests, such as advertising and TV executives.

Fender – Guitar invented by Leo Fender and the rest was – wah, wah, wah wah, wah wah, wah wah wah, wah wah wah wah scratch scratch scratch – just fantastic. The Fender Strat or Stratocaster was played badly by millions, brilliantly by dozens, including Hank Marvin and Jimi Hendrix. Fender players are rarely Gibson players (and vice versa) as they have distinctly different characteristics.

F*** off – International expression of annoyance towards another person, or friendly greeting of surprise between British roadies and musos. As good as five lagers for male bonding if used with wit, subtlety and a friendly smile.

Gaffer tape – Mystical substance that can do anything: repair truck exhausts, hold up trousers, mend speakers, etc.

The gear – Musical equipment required for a rock concert; or, for the occasional fans of sixties movies and purveyors of sixties kitsch, illicit drugs.

The get in or load in – The time that the door of a venue opens for the crew to start setting up the gear.

Hit man – Any record company executive, high-ranking enough, or smart enough, to grab the glory on the fleeting occasions when there is any to grab.

Humpers – Gear carriers, the camels of the industry

and accorded much the same lack of respect; supposedly provided on the rider by the promoter at each venue. The seasoned crew boss will ask for twenty if he requires ten. That way, when only five appear he won't be completely knackered getting the gear up and ready by soundcheck.

The King – Elvis Presley. The announcement "Elvis has left the building" has passed into legendary rock parlance for any situation in which the audience is still shouting for its stars after they have managed to sneak out of the building without being mobbed.

Label – Record label, presumably because originally labels were glued on to 78s.

Leader – Splicing tape found in those studios which have engineers old enough to recall the glory days of musicians who could play.

Les Paul – The famous guitar invented by Les Paul.

Liggers – People who attend gigs without paying, often rock journalists, their friends and family. In fact, anyone backstage the band wishes weren't.

Marshall – Amplifier that has a volume control which goes all the way to ten, unless customised.

Midi Hell – The place you go when you open your MIDI software application. The mantra goes like this: "It was working a minute ago..."

Mix – a) Last stage in the recording process when different performances are balanced and given their final polish; b) what happens when the sound engineer, thanks to advice from the producer, turns your great performance into a good one.

MOR – Middle of the Road. Another radio format, rather than a dodgy place to sit.

Monitors – On stage, the loudspeakers for monitoring sound; in a studio, the TV set for monitoring the visuals; at school, the person who stopped future rock musicians from nicking everyone else's milk.

Musicians, Musos – Those who play musical instruments and live with people who have real jobs.

Overdubs – The part of the recording process that guitarists love and that takes forever, or until the money runs out.

P.A. – Public address system or, if the star is successful, a personal assistant.

Pluggers – Those who promote records to radio. "Have you heard the new Smeggies record? It's at 212 this week, but it's a No. 1. I know it's 9 minutes long but it will really fit in with your programming."

Pop – Word sometimes inaccurately used as entirely interchangeable with rock. This is the kindergarten of rock, aimed primarily at the youngest sector of the record buying public. The Beatles were pop. The Stones are rock.

Punters – Those who pay for a ticket, go to see the band, and may or may not get a result. Also known by agents and concert promoters as 'bums on seats' or 'the count'.

Recording artist – The one whose name is credited on the front of the CD. See Artists.

Residuals – Royalties you can claim to regularly receive when you need to borrow money.

Rider – Extravagant (or, more commonly, not) wish-list of goodies to be provided at venues by the promoter, normally at the artist's expense. Can also specify items not to be provided, as per David Lee Roth's tongue-in-cheek alleged request for "Smarties, but no orange ones".

Riggers – Highly insured persons who rig lights.

Run through – TV rehearsal where the camera people are unfortunately obliged to follow the director's intentions.

Session – Traditionally a three hour stint, but hey, this is rock 'n roll, anything goes.

Session player – A musician who records sessions with anyone who pays him cheques that shouldn't bounce.

Soundcheck – What the band believe to be rehearsal time, but the sound engineer knows to be his only opportunity to check that all instruments balance before the punters arrive and ruin the satisfying curves of their graphic equalizers. Often the time when rows will break out if things aren't running smoothly.

Spinal Tap – Band name from painfully humorous spoof documentary of the same title. Astonishing for its unnerving accuracy.

Spondoolies or **Gliders** – Roadie-speak for money in a currency not native. Usually reserved for *per diems* (daily expenses).

Venue – Concert hall, or gig, but rarely a show, unless you wish to be regarded as a Lloyd Webber fan, or you're a jobbing strummer in a musical.

THE AUTHOR

David Knopfler, founder and former member of Dire Straits, was born in Glasgow, and grew up in Newcastle-upon-Tyne. With a guitar and piano in his bedroom and a drum kit at age 11, by 14 he was performing his own songs in folk clubs. He cannot recall any other aspirations beyond writing songs, composing and playing music.

The owner of various rag-tag-and-bobtail publishing and record companies, a former rock manager (never again), composer of scores for film and television, occasional rock journalist and habitual internet geek, he currently enjoys a solo recording career (with seven albums to date). For these he has increasingly garnered excellent reviews, perfectly mirroring his decreasing sales. In the less wilfully self-deluded this might be seen as a problem.

An apparent authority on home-grown organic vegetables, he lives happily with his wife and son in the English countryside where he has a recording studio and slowly notches up an impressive list of writing credits. His neighbours remain hopeful he may yet retire.